NEDÍ NEZŲ

GOOD MEDICINE

ᎤᏂ ᎤᏓ

NEDÍ NEZǪ

GOOD MEDICINE

ᎤᏅ ᎤᎦ

poems

TENILLE K. CAMPBELL

ARSENAL PULP PRESS
VANCOUVER

ARSENAL PULP PRESS
Suite 202 – 211 East Georgia St.
Vancouver, BC V6A 1Z6
Canada
arsenalpulp.com

The publisher gratefully acknowledges the support of the Canada Council for the Arts and the British Columbia Arts Council for its publishing program, and the Government of Canada, and the Government of British Columbia (through the Book Publishing Tax Credit Program), for its publishing activities.

Arsenal Pulp Press acknowledges the xʷməθkʷəy̓əm (Musqueam), Sḵwx̱wú7mesh (Squamish), and səl̓ilwətaɁɬ (Tsleil-Waututh) Nations, custodians of the traditional, ancestral, and unceded territories where our office is located. We pay respect to their histories, traditions, and continuous living cultures and commit to accountability, respectful relations, and friendship.

The following poems have been previously published: a version of "I make love," *Briarpatch*, December 27, 2018; "I wonder" under the title "questions," *PRISM international*, April 23, 2019; "sex sex sex" under the title "medicine songs," *PRISM international* 57.3, Spring 2019; a version of "thick indigenous women," *Walrus*, February 21, 2020; versions of "water so clear" and "red rose hot tea on my tongue," *ndncountry*, *Contemporary Verse 2: The Canadian Journal of Poetry and Critical Writing* 41.2, Fall 2018, 211–12; a version of "we met in late spring," "A Life Built Together: Photographer Captures the 'Grace of Growing Old with Someone,'" CBC News, February 16, 2019; and the English version of "you kiss" under the title "3 Poems," *The Peak: Reproductive Justice* 57.3, Spring 2018, 14–15.

Cover and text design by Jazmin Welch
Cover beadwork by Heather Dickson
Edited by Caitlin Ward
Copy edited by Shirarose Wilensky
Proofread by Alison Strobel

Printed and bound in Canada

Library and Archives Canada Cataloguing in Publication:
Title: Nedí nezų = Good medicine : poems / Tenille K. Campbell.
Other titles: Good medicine
Names: Campbell, Tenille K., author.
Description: Text in English with some text in Cree and Dene.
Identifiers: Canadiana (print) 20200324527 | Canadiana (ebook) 20200324772 | ISBN 9781551528465 (softcover) | ISBN 9781551528472 (HTML)
Subjects: LCGFT: Poetry.
Classification: LCC PS8605.A5494 N43 2021 | DDC C811/.6—dc23

for omeasoo and heather,
for adar and erica,
for maral and nazanine,
for karen and brittany,
for chelsea and michelle,
for dakota and tasha

for the women
who have held me close
taught me well
and let me be free

nuhëghanila
I love you

kinanāskomitināwāw
I am thankful to all of you

contents

1
LANGUAGE LESSONS

2
NORTHERN LIGHTS

3
BROKEN TREATIES

4
THE LAND

1
LANGUAGE LESSONS

snagging while Indigenous
means road trips from
rez to rez
one hundred miles
a story in the making
meeting grandparents
cousins and aunties
because there are no secrets
among family

snagging while Indigenous
means bringing dry meat
across borders
jars of canned fish
clinking in the back seat
bags of frozen blueberries
waiting to be handed to relations
ancient bribes for modern flirtations

snagging while Indigenous
means DMs and double taps
and casually saying hey
I was just in the neighbourhood
we should hang out
I know your cousin

you look like trouble
and you know it
tall and lean
head cocked just so
I can taste you already
    northern accent dripping
    from tongue and lips

you look like morning regrets
the shuffling of clothes
the lost bra
the headache
trying to remember
    where I am
    what your name is

you look like
someone who will text
that I'm beautiful
    captivating like northern lights
    sparkling like a blanket of stars
like someone
who has those words
    on copy and paste

you are fresh river water
chilled by underwater glacial
pulsing through my mouth
over my tongue
down my throat
carrying story

kissing cree boys
around spinning bottles
snaps never posted

stories told in group chats and DMs
nēhiyaw to dënësųłıné
smiling turning into laughter
turning into speculative glances
you kiss me

like you wanna remember how I taste
imprinting your lips onto mine
making sure I never forget
these early mornings late nights
who's keeping track
all I know is

when you pull me closer hand on neck
grinning and making me blush

I almost forget
it's just a game

when you kneel down to worship
palms laid flat on soft thighs
head bowed in praise
speak out loud the blessings before you
say my name with reverence

when your lips and tongue
taste me for the first time
knees spread before you
know that
we are in ceremony

when you feel me break
body trembling spilling joy
hand reaching for you
drawing you in
remember this moment

I've never wanted to dance
the drums don't call me home
swirling ribbons and colourful beads
have never entangled me
we don't all powwow, you know

but
but
but
watching you
big drum singer
I want to dance
for you

between thick pale thighs
you called me a feast
making me gush with words
and a tongue licking clit
sucking marrow from bone

you were thirsty
and my desire
quenched you

I want to taste your language
as you whisper it into my mouth
let my tongue lick and suck
your vowels and consonants

you make me
wanna slow dance
under moonlight and snowflakes
hand tangled in your hair
led down into heartbreak
and hope

make me your fry bread
make me your indian corn soup
make me your candied salmon
make me your strawberry anything
feast on me

morning stretches
hands above my hand
back arching
breasts bare
nipples hard in the morning chill
your body warm beside me
already hard
already wet

mood

it's that two a.m. DM
between blackfoot and dene
a casual hook   a smooth reply
and now

I know how you like it when we
    feast
I know the curve of your
    smile
I know how you look when you
    smudge

a few well-placed words
a snapchat streak
we just making relations
traditional-like

you smelled of sweat
lumber shavings
dust and nature
lay on the crevices
of your skin
    i n h a l e   t h e m
rub against them
letting your scent
mark me
as territory
taken

saltwater crush
feet dangling off the pier
flip-flops barely hanging on
prairie wonder
over vastness

you bring me to the water
hand in hand
pointing out the landmarks of your memories
deep blue stories
of another people

words sit unfamiliar
upon clumsy tongues
and I smile

tell me again
teach me more

I don't want this
crushed feeling
barely breathing
cheeks burning
smile can't stop torture this is
torture

how will you know
unless you try?

spare me the cliché

he doesn't call
he doesn't text
he doesn't snap
he doesn't DM
he doesn't creep

this is a one-sided story
where my name
doesn't cross his mind
and I can't stop thinking
about his smile
phone in hand
don't text
don't text

I text

I sit on his lap
letting him whisper off
tank and bra
letting him taste
neck and lips and breasts
watching him leave
strawberry stains behind
I lean back to
take off feather earrings
"keep them on"
he makes me moan
   savage

she tells me
she loves my rose lips
as she strokes my feathers
glittering nails brushing
against bared skin
making me shiver
leaning in
"can I kiss you?"
she makes me feel
   savage

house party
some random stairway
he cradles my jaw
in his hands
tracing my lips
with his
softly pulling
at wild earrings
"you look real sexy
with feathers"
he makes me ache
   savage

kissing indigenous
means thick lips grinning
the smell of ski-doos running
campfire smoke clinging
the taste of tea still on your lips
love bites on necks
hands roaming under jackets
and cuddling into them
head ducked down
smiling so hard
that you never remember
why you were sad

it was quiet
soft dawn
birds just waking
sun just warming
you lay with me
brown nipples soft
on delicate breasts
one hickey
bruised and hot
lipstick smeared
flesh marked
desire sated
my nails tracing
hips for days
goosebumps
you smiled
eyes closed
babe stop
you whispered
hips arching
towards my hands
as I pulled away
I giggle
start all over
again

do you even remember
how to love?

do you remember
how to love anyone?

he asked me this
late one night
my leg draped over his hips
breathing slow and steady
cuddled up
after a night of play and
language lessons

I grinned

he didn't know
I never cuddled

kikaskēyihtān cī
tānisīsi ta sākihiyan

kikiskisin
tānisīsi ta sākihēt awiyak

ē-kwēcimit
pēyakwāw kā tipiskāk
niskāt mēkwāc kā ohpinahk
pēyahtak ēhēyahk
ē-ciminitoyahk
kā kīsi mētawēyahk
ē-kiskinohamātoyahk pīkiskwēwin

nipāhpisin

namōya kiskēyihtam
namōya wīhkac niciminawak

you sit on my couch
rubbing my feet
toenails painted
your favourite shade of blue
teasing me
about my fear of commitment

I'm ready, you say
and I look away
you ask
what if someone steals me?

and I laugh

sechuzeh
if someone steals you
you were looking to go
you can't take
what doesn't want to be taken

you may be ready
twenty-six and kid-less
looking for that forever kind of love
starlight and saná?á ahhenít'ı
in your eyes

I've had that kind of love
the madness of it all
I've made a life with someone
believed the dreams and the lies
and watched him get
stolen

I've hurt and ached and cried
and fought to be this woman
feet lying across
her younger lover
toenails painted detł'és
his favourite colour
laughing
over the threat of losing

sechuzeh
you're already gone
you just don't know it

2
NORTHERN LIGHTS

falling into like
makes my rez accent thick
my laughter loud
and my hair toss epic

falling into like
makes my eyeliner sharp
my lips glossy
and my earrings savage

falling into lust
makes my underwear silky
my t-shirts low
and my cleavage glittery

falling into lust
makes my scent tantalizing
my smile coy
and my hands searching

falling into love
lays me bare
waking in a room
filled with the light of dawn
smiling at you
burying my face in a pillow
as you pull me close

kiss me
and tell me I'm beautiful

we've seen sunsets
and sunrises
rolling in blankets
heartbeats racing
fighting the coming light

I want
to walk hand in hand
in the daytime
fingers laced
shoulders leaning into
each other
pulse racing
hair tucked behind one ear
smiling to myself
for myself

you are the sun
I the earth
potent waiting able
seeking your heat
season after season

but we hide
between sunset and sunrise
under a pale moon
we breathe softly
not breaking soft treaties

sometimes
we need the night

I whisper your name in the dark
sitting under bridges beside cornfields

I let your sounds roll up my throat
over my tongue through my teeth
I call you into memories and a thousand stories
how you kissed the inside of my thigh
how you bit my neck before sucking
how you held my arms above my head
how you fucked me deep

my nipples get hard when I think of you
when I moan your name
under bridges beside cornfields
all the places we fucked

I whisper your name
everywhere

I wanna be tangled in moonlight
wrapped up in northern lights
guided home by the North Star
trailing down Churchill River
hand in hand with you

I wanna be tracing your stories
constellations of ink and scars
hearing your memories
echo in the dark
between dusk and dawn

I wanna be your roots ensnared
in sandy soil lush with moss
beside hidden waterfalls
soft rock smoothed over
by running water

I wanna be part of your joy
the smile on your face
when you hear my name
the blush in your cheeks
when you think of last night

I wanna be your home
your land
your memories

sweetgrass
embers burning
in a cracked yellow bowl
bought from a vintage shop
a thousand years ago
hands holding
rainy Vancouver
smiling in the damp and grey
because you smell like
coffee and cigarette smoke
you smelled like
home
accent thick
as you told me
how you welded towers
saw the city
from a different view
smile wide
as you listened
to my stories
of a day at home
laundry dishes cleaning
hands warm
as you handed me
a smooth yellow bowl
just bought from a vintage shop
because yellow
is my favourite colour

the first time I fell in love
I fell fearlessly
heart tumbling laughter echoing
fingers laced together on moon-filled nights
your tongue teaching mine
new ways to say neghąnıtą

the first time I fell in love
I met your family
sitting around a kitchen table
ears warm cheeks burning
they told me stories of you
they told me the beginning of you

the first time neghąnıtą hesjá
your fingers discovered me
waking desire
my first moans cresting in heavy shadows
legs spread dripping wet
body learning
new ways to say I love you

the first time I fell in love
I gave you all my wild and reckless

kǫndue deneghąnıtą hurésĵle

listening to songs
that remind me of the North
crowded dance floors
two-stepping beer in hand
friends' laughter surrounding
your arms around me
your voice in my ear

you kissed
like the northern lights
lips and tongue dancing
in ancient precision
capturing me
like a child
who whistles
at the unknown

you tasted
like morning fog
late nights and low moans
rye and coke cigarette smoke
you tasted
like her man
I wondered
would you think of me
the next time you tasted her

listening to songs
that remind me of the North
black coffee and blue mornings
regrets in the ache of my lips
that still feel you

do you think of her
when you are so at home
between my thighs
my accent thick in your ears
nezy

do you think of her
when you let me kiss your neck
leaving lipstick and love marks
on your flesh

when I take you in my mouth
and you moan
head rolled back
hands fisted in my hair

when you caress my breast
biting oh so softly
just to hear me gasp

do you think of her
when you tell me
you're single?

the first time I kissed you
I had to stand on tiptoes
hands on your shoulders
calf muscles stretching

I didn't tell you then
but you reminded me of sekóę

we were under street light
your arms gently holding me close
you bit my lip   grinning   how did you know
I like some pain with my pleasure

I didn't tell you then
but you made me degharé nałtsel
Beaver River style

sleeping with you
was like riding a canoe down treacherous rapids
someone's gonna get hurt

midsummer moments
holding hands at street fairs
leaning into you as you told me
honi I pretended to believe

I watched you behind sunglasses
as you borrowed money for drinks

we were lying in bed
I slowly dragged nails up and down
your back   your breathing deepened
minute by minute

you had told me you were starting
to like me I counted the number of times
I let you meet my friends family   daughter

you didn't know
it was the last night
you would sleep over

I count to three
breathing deep
I remember your touch
on my neck
lips   breasts   thighs

I count to three
closing my eyes
I hear your laughter
chest rumbling as you held me
close

I count to three
pressing my lips together
I still taste
your smile as you kissed me
good morning

I count to three
biting my lip
I can hear your voice still
    I'm sorry

pēyak
nīso
nisto

pēyak
nīṣo
nisto

pēyak
nīso
nisto

pēyak
nīso
nisto

the last time we kissed

you pushed my body against the deck wall
I remember the scratchy wood at my back
you pulled my hips closer to yours
fingers against my skin making me ache
you still tasted like last night of laughter and drinks
and I fell into lust again and again and again
moaning against your mouth
my arms around your neck
pulling you in deeper harder faster
I ran fingernails through your sunshine blond hair
the sky reflecting the colour of your eyes
looking into mine and I had to
look away grinning blushing dripping
you make me
feel all the ways I don't wanna feel
and I know that was the last time
because I won't watch you walk away anymore

it was the quiet moments
between us
that made me fall off the ledge
into the northern lights
chasing dene accents
over tundra through taiga
stumbling over broken stars
and broken promises

you didn't look back
didn't see me trip
fall down and cut myself
on the stories
of how I used to love you

the snow crackled in the cold
sun dogs danced with ice crystals
you were so far in the distance
you didn't see
someone else's hand
reach down and help me up

you didn't see
when I stopped falling for you

you're that broken
retelling
of a story
we struggle to remember
lost in the stuttering
of an actual name
of a remembered feeling
of a triumph
long forgotten
and all we can do
is laugh

the silence killed us
four-hour car rides
looking out the window
   from prairie grass and skinny poplars
   to evergreens and muskeg
hands wrapped just so
to make every part of intimacy
unavailable to you

I don't wanna do this
    anymore

the fight is gone
          it too sits quiet

broken hearts turn into numb smiles
because everyone is watching
waiting to say I told you so
I wonder how long I will stay
leaving is just as lonely

I remember how I ached
when my reserve came into sight
we drove onto the grounds
where we had talked all night
made love for the first time
fell into this relationship

teasing laughter and thick accents
guiding the way

only silence now
pulling bags and baby from truck
kissing you goodbye
eyes staring up at the northern lights
as you continued on

I didn't know why I was so sad
only that it felt like an ending

3
BROKEN
TREATIES

indigenous academia

makes me ache
talk with me
I want to hear
vowels dripping
from your tongue
mix in the words
from your nation
it doesn't matter
I don't yet understand
I will learn

we're coming in waves
passing stories
where we've been and
where we're going
a hidden library nook
a quiet reading room
a safe place to let go
surrounded with people
who laugh like you
old travel knowledge
for new ways

we're reclaiming space
singing songs from the land
low notes echoing
down hallways
hand drum on your lap
long lean fingers tapping
the beat you constantly hear
making me dream
beyond ivory towers

we're taking it
making it
visibly
undeniably
irrevocably
indigenous

I make love
under Indian Acts
my womb
a political battleground
don't cum in me
I don't need the reminder
dripping
that we are not compatible

you fit so nicely
between thick fry bread thighs
dimpled and soft
ready to be devoured
your hands tease dark nipples
to a cranberry flush
arching towards the air
you centre yourself on my
womanhood
and wait for my natural depths
to welcome you in
never mind
that you were never
supposed to be here
in the first place

professor
I watch you
education dripping off tongue
four five six syllable words
acknowledging lands
in your element
sharing knowledge
speaking truths
with a grin and a laugh
I wonder
what your smile will look like
in the morning

your hand squeezing gently
just under my jaw
fingers wrapped around my throat
pushing me back onto bed
forcing my hands to headboard
kneeling between my legs
making me look away
heat on my cheeks
dominant to my submissive

and I sigh

finally

sadness drenched in dripping syrup
torn into bite-sized pieces
                        you don't wanna
c h o k e

how does my loneliness taste
boiled raspberries
over vanilla
ice cream
how does my anger taste
sweet flesh of white
fish smoked over an
open fire
how does my assault taste
                        smoked dry meat
smeared with salt
and butter

but this is a ceremony for one
all you get
are empty buckets
smelling of smudge and smoke

do you think of me
late at night
flipping through your phone
your friends
they don't know about us
they double tap each poem
how often
do you see our stories
on your timeline

it's summer, babe
a time for remember whens
blaming it on late nights
and the neon moon
it's festivals and laughter
live bands and pitchers of beer
it's when we started

I should unblock your number

repeat

you were a repeat

a number I never blocked

repeat

the way you made love

falling down my body

mouth seeking pussy

repeat

hands spreading thighs

my giggles in the night

you still talk too much

repeat

licking and loving

your way into me

asking me to say your name

repeat

mouth constantly moving

over my body over my lips

speaking lies into truth

repeat

the way you watched me

get dressed never leaving

anything behind

repeat

kissing you one last time
with dawn lighting streets
car keys in hand

goodbye

men are trash
ring hiding DM deleting
never gonna meet my family
kind of basic bro
who wanna be the pēyak
wanna be the main one
wanna be the inspiration
for that next line in the next poem
never mind
you're already somebody else's
dream come true
why ain't that enough for you?

men are trash
head between thighs
feasting celebrating
only to tell me
how you like my insta story
how you wanna be
in my poetry
how do you like your poem, baby?

men are trash
from the I never cum this fasts
to the I'll never hit you agains
when a native woman's laughter
grows sharp sharing story spilling tea
recognizing ceremony
healing laughing criticizing
reminding each other
we are worth more

one guy
he made sweet sweet love to me hands caressing my face lips
softly touching mine I wanted him to go faster deeper harder
but he respected women so we made love missionary style gen-
tly sighing in the dark his orgasm soft and slow

afterwards he held me in his arms tilted my chin up and whispered
by the way, I'm a fan I love your poetry

one guy
I urged him closer through every text and double tap on his
instagram I wanted him hands in mine lips on mine imagining
what he would be like between sheets how he would smile when
I would moan only his name but he told me he loved the idea
of me his idealization of me

his indigenous lover wannabe
        he didn't want to ruin it, you see

these guys
they read my words see my lips they always see my lips and I'm
supposed to be flattered humbled someone wants me fat me
thick me supposed to take it love it they imagine me before they
have me never mind they don't even know me

but they like my poems, you see

black velvet sky
dying stars flicking dreams
we walked beneath
yellow street lamps
full moon
you told me about
northern lights
you don't whistle
because you don't want to get caught

we in the south now
leave your hands open
in this ocean of prairie grass
don't ask for help
at farmers' fields
on stolen lands
on empty streets
ghost cars around every corner

romance is lighting my smoke
goodbye kisses holding my hand
watching you walk away
so red and blues
don't stop you
before you get home

when you come to the door
black garbage bag in hand
full of clothes and mismatched socks
underwear she bought you
t-shirts your mom got you
I realize
loving you
would mean loving me less

I fought too hard
to be this version of me
and I'm not raising
a grown-ass man
again

you want me to celebrate you
as I have done in the past
to honour your Indigenous blood
high cheekbones and soft thick lips

but in case you forgot, babe
honour isn't a two a.m. DM
a grainy dick pic half hard
dirty laundry on the floor
honour ain't kissing me
going home to your gf
and calling me a mistake

you want me to honour you
laugh and giggle
about how you bang the drum
smoke the moose meat
and how big your erect tipi is

you want our joy
our love our laughter
you want our medicine
the strength we bring home
the comfort we give
you want it all

but tell me
where did your honour go?

the night we met I fell in love
with the character you played
the white buffalo the unicorn
the wet dream in Indigenous form
language dripping fry bread glistening
beads dazzling lips grinning
nīcimos
             you made me believe

you didn't lie I already knew you
my heart tripping along falling laughing
I wrote from nothing

so first dates mean last dates
secret girlfriends showing up
amidst bathroom chats and knowing eyes
secret DMs in secret apps
I might still have your dick pics
but she's sitting in your lap

the night we met I fell in love
with the character you played
    but really
    who got played

you wouldn't have fit in on the rez
auntie looking at you like a snack
brother watching you for signs of colonization
your loafers getting dusty off gravel roads
discreetly dusting them in between visits and polite
laughter between thin lips and clenched teeth

you wouldn't have fit in on the rez
bannock and jam sitting untouched
moose meat stew growing cold in faded bowls
you're the type to say no thanks
when food is handed to you
cross your knees fold your palms in
don't touch don't touch don't touch

you wouldn't have fit in on the rez
wondering why we don't get a hotel
even as you smile at my family
who share feast and home with you
even as you count the minutes
until we can leave

you wouldn't have fit in on the rez

the first time we fuck
I can't say make love
I don't know who your family are
but the first time we fuck
I expect
you to bless my sex
with prayers straight from your mouth
I want you to whisper your truths
with tongue
up and down my sacred being
where my moon and sun collide
where my power patiently waits

the first time we fuck
you need to recognize the ceremony
that my body holds
I'm your sweat lodge
bringing you closer to the sky people
eyes closed forehead against mine
I ground you to the earth
hands braced on either side of me
fingers clenched tight as I tighten around you

the first time we fuck
you need to recognize your blessings
hold me in your arms fingers trailing
curves the Creator made to hold power
feel my heart beat slow breathing deep
before you slip out of bed
covering me with soft blankets

the first time we fuck
you may recognize
the possibility within me
a safe place to land a welcoming
but understand this
I may be your ceremony
but my bed is not your home

I wonder
if you would love me

if my thighs had gaps
to let in the setting sun

if my curves were rolling hills and shallow lakes
instead of mountains and oceans

if my skin ran smooth over muscles
instead of water rippling over rapids

I wonder
if you would love me

if my bones were delicate and hollow
sustained only on your compliments

if my stomach lay flat and unscarred
untouched by birth and life

if my feet were tiny like a hummingbird's
instead of flat and wide to grip the earth

I wonder
if you would love me

if my breasts were a dainty handful
instead of spilling through your fingers

if my mouth was only used for your pleasure
instead of reciting poetry aimed to cut

if my mind only thought of you
setting aside decolonization and language reclamation

I wonder if you would love me
if I wasn't me at all

I am not a wild strawberry
dessert to be feasted upon
perfectly fit for your hand
perfectly fit for your tongue

I am the prickly hazelnut
barbs deep and invisible under skin
a constant reminder not to touch
but you know I'm worth it

I am not the flower that bends in the wind
content to be one of many
petals dancing in a rippling field
your visual indulgence your wildflower

I am the evergreen with fading needles
roots deep in sandy soils
slightly burned from ancient fires
a home to only the survivors

I am not the field where you make a home
protecting you from the elements
quenching your thirst in my spring waters
staking your claim in my hills

I am the jagged cliffs of northern waterfalls
painted upon generations ago
carrying stories from a past
you pretend doesn't exist

why indigenous erotica
why not just erotica
do you do it different
do you do it special

officially:
indigenous erotica
acknowledges the intersectional space
of political and social influences
external pressures
and internal dialogue
that occurs when indigenous people
engage in activities with sexual and sensual overtones

unofficially:
when we fuck
the frogs go silent
to listen to our mating breaths
the northern lights dance
when we reach our peak
the wolves howl at the full moon
rejoicing in our orgasms

when we fuck
our skin glistens
like the star people we are
our lips moan
ancient languages understood
our hands trace
petroglyphs on our bare backs

when we fuck
all indigenous and shit
we lie in each other's arms
heartbeats matching dreams mingling
mink blankets surround us
the scent of sweetgrass embraces us
and we are safe
for that one moment

that's why
we erotica indigenous

4
THE
LAND

I'm tired of thin pointy lips
lips that cut and hiss
their right for chief wahoo and redskins
lips that say
they don't see race
everyone is equal
and won't I be their
naughty squaw

I want thick lips
that taste of dry meat
and glisten with butter
lips that kiss under pine trees
and tell me they love me
in accents from the land
I want Dene lips Cree lips
Metis lips Mohawk lips and Anishinabe lips
I want Mi'kmaq lips and Stó:lō lips
I want lips that are thick
with stories and sweetness
thick lips moose lips
I want
blueberry cloud lips

you kiss
like the North
lips devouring every
wild inch of me
tongue tasting
lightly feasting
finding every
delicious curve

I am neckbones
and you
are hungry

nentsun dé

hotie yatthé ges?o

nedhá seghą nesué yełtsį

netthú ?a senarıdlı

tsełı?aze ?a beghanedheré

toryu setthik'e daı hekum kanıtá?o

si neckbones

hesłı nen bebéthı

I want to kiss
dënësułıné
back into your skin
lips to your shoulder
nails tracing kinship
down your back
down to your feet
where you are grounded in us

I want to give you ceremony
under gentle moons and watchful stars
I want you to moan nezų
taste the language on your tongue
as you enter me
I want my ehaskëth
to be your first taste
of our oldest medicine

lie in my bed
under thick mink blankets
arms curled around you
tracing features
them dene naghé from black lake
cheekbones from fond du lac
those lips from la loche
helch'ul from patuanak
don't you know you are one of us
neʔá nohonıʔë nechá

come back to us
sehel hıgąl

water so clear
the rocks shimmer
free of moss
glittering with
crystalline sand
and broken sediment

I want you
to float down
my ancestors' river
feel the sun
on your shoulders
gaze at me
hand dipped in
cool river water
remembering the
heartbeat of
home

I want you
to pull canoe
from wet pathways
muscles straining
pulling us in
to safe lands
that carry
my stories

we stand at shorelines
embedded in history
feet dipped in
a never freezing river
and I wait
for your hand
to reach for mine

come home with me

red rose hot tea on my tongue
campfire smoke and poplar leaves
playing in the wind
your hand in mine
I lean back
lift my face to the sky
close my eyes
smile at the sweet
beginnings
blooming around me

sitting on rocky earth
listening to you speak
mimicking the sounds
rolling your ancestors' words
out of throat and through teeth
you smile and lean in
repeating repeating repeating

I love how you
teach me
mouth soft upon mine
whispering love words
I don't understand
into my being sharing breath
and I can't help the burning
heat across cheeks
you make me ache
like the land beneath us
lying in wait
holding story

you dipped
your fingers
into my body
tracing the entrance
to ecstasy
until your finger
was marked
by moon

you tasted me
letting me sit
upon your tongue
like the first moose kill
when the blood
is thick and hot
sweet like syrup
scooped by hand
from deep within
you honour that time
by feasting upon flesh
sipping blood
and giving thanks

welcome to the hunt

your fingers lace in mine
you tell me about the hunting trips
shooting a mōswa
the ache in your shoulders
as you carve and carry flesh
from maskēkohk to kotowān
to the cardboard-laden
kitchen floors of grandmas and mamas
aunts and cousins
kāsisin mohkomān
glistening under weather-beaten hands
as they finish
what you started

you lift my hand up
to kiss my open palm
and I tingle
wondering if you know
kīko mācīwin
ē-itōtamān mēkwāc

my body holds wells of water
spilling over rock and sandy soil
my heartbeat is the call of loons
the croaking of frogs at dusk
my kiss is the silence at nightfall
the yipping howl of coyotes in the dark

my body is soft muskeg
when you touch me I give
fingers sink deep into earth
soft and wet

you trace my land formations at night
licking freckle to beauty mark
tracing history flesh to flesh

invisible boundaries divide me
before you and after you

thick indigenous women
are spilled beads and tangled thread
worth the time to pick up to untangle

we are curves spilling stories
against your lips
our thighs are soft muskeg
protecting good medicines
our skin soft as tanned hide
caress us with care
as you are touching
our ancestors' wildest dreams

thick indigenous women
are the feast during a long winter
canned raspberries fresh bannock
warm butter leaking between your fingers
come and eat

we hold joy in every round shoulder
laugh loudly drawing all eyes
we squeeze against you
and you hold us tight
smiling at your blessings

because thick indigenous women
we are magic and if you aren't careful
someone else will pick up spilled beads
and untangle threads

with you
I wanna watch
the smoke curl
from burning sage
little red embers
heating medicine
casting blessings
you make me feel
like I can wear a ribbon skirt
sit outside a drum circle
not touch power
during my moon time

with you
I think I can sit and listen
mouth nëhıyawëwın
as you teach me language
teach me ceremony
ignoring the ache
dënësułıné words
pushing up my throat

with you
I wanna lie on prairie grass
open blue skies and warm winds
listen to your laughter
echo with your ancestors
never telling you
how setsuné
shared stories
from her grandmothers
travelling to the south
trading pemmican, making kin
you would never believe me
you think this
has always been nêhiyaw askiy

with you
who only sees sweat lodges and sweetgrass
who doesn't see the blood
in urban experience and off-reserve living

with you
who practises spiritually
but not practically
I could almost pretend
could almost sit back
step one beat behind
almost

call me auntie

I am one hundred and ninety-five
moons older than you

I am one child born of me
older than you

I am one million tears of sadness and laughter
older than you

call me auntie

I remember
how you wanted
to take me home
to your lands
show me northern ways
get me beading
trapping cleaning fishing
make a good woman
out of me

I thought
I already was one

urban Indigenous
flirting with traditionalist
means biting my tongue
because asking you to check yourself
equals lectures on gender roles
you don't understand
matriarchs come from everywhere
and this is all native land

spare me your teaching
when I comment about the weather
miss me with the gifts of medicines
bearing sweet shame
and gentle condemnation
I can't walk with you in a good way
just recognize the teachings I bring
do you see the story between humble attitudes
and broken hearts left on sidewalks

I don't walk in circles with the sun
know how to pray palms up
but that don't mean I don't see the ceremony
that my body holds skirt or no skirt
my feet still touch the ground
connecting me to mine concrete or grass
latte in hand and lip gloss glittering
still Indigenous

if I wore braids tightly plaited in two rows
rocked a skirt ribbons brightly flashing
would I be more worthy
of your attention
I like my hair wild
laughing too loud flirting too much
to never look you in the eye
          can you admit   you like watching me

we aren't all nice aunties
open arms and kind smiles
we don't all bake bannock
keep secret stores of dry meat
and fresh blueberries

some of us are called mean
our tongue spares no one
fools tremble before us
some of us are called city
we live under skyscrapers
walk in ivory towers with ivory people
some of us are too much
too loud too real
it's hard to take our love

but an auntie is an auntie
and the mean ones
tell truth you don't want to hear
and the nice ones
hold you when you break
and the quiet ones
keep secrets whispered in the dark
and the loud ones
match your wild stories
and the elderly ones
watch us all
remembering the aunties
who came before

she makes me feel
        traditional
ribbon skirt swaying
sage burning   water boiling
ready for a
        feast

let me clean your strawberries
rinse them with spring water
gently pick away the stems
fingertips stained soft pink
licking the juice
running down fingers
don't waste a drop

we met in late spring
the ground was damp and soft
by the next moon
my heart was his

right now
we hold hands under city lights
and walk on concrete
when he smiles
I see echoes of the Elder
he will be

I imagine
walking down a rez road
hand in hand
a bucket full of blueberries
to be picked and cleaned

I see a life of road trips
country music as he sings along
hand in hand across the seats
sitting in a thousand stories
and remember whens

I see brown babies and late nights
birthday parties and cousins running wild
days at the beach evenings on the boat
always and always
hand in hand

I want to watch your wrinkles deepen
under the passing full moons
I want to see grey hairs appear
and strong shoulders stoop
as our families grow

I will tell our grandchildren
we met in late spring

sex sex sex
one-trick pony she is
>> baby
>> I got tricks
>> for generations
the biggest trick
is still being here
surviving thriving organizing

we still here

we echo and ripple descendants pouring
down concrete over pavement
babies cradled on hips snug within cradleboards
wrapped in starblankets under protest signs
#JusticeForColten
#TinaFontaine
#IndigenousResistance

we don't have the luxury
of not explaining to our babies
why we don't wear black hoodies
why we don't take cabs alone
and why we don't trust cops

but

we still here
hands holding mukluk wearing
tears spilling laughter flowing
medicine in our very bones
ancestors in our eyes
as we gaze and catch feelings
across citywide marches
seeing us in them and them in us
just tricks
surviving thriving organizing
yeah
we got tricks for days

GLOSSARY

dene

degharé nałtsel: it was really wet

dene naghé: Dene/people's eyes

dënësułıné: Dene People/Dene language

detł'és: blue

ehaskëth: orgasm

helch'ul: their smile

honi: story/stories

kǫndue deneghąnıtą hurésı́le: I don't want to love someone like
that anymore

neʔá nohonıʔë nechá: because of you our story is big

nedı́ nezų: good medicine

neghąnıtą: I love you

neghąnıtą hesjá: I started to fall in love with you

nezų: good

sanáʔá ahhenı́t'ı: beautiful sunset

sechuzeh: my sweetheart

sehel hıgąl: come with me

sekóę: my home

setsuné: grandmother

cree

ē-itōtamān mēkwāc: I'm doing right now

kāsisin mohkomān: sharp knife

kīko mācīwin: what kind of hunting

kotowān: campfire

maskēkohk: muskeg

mōswa: moose

nēhiyaw: Cree People

nêhiyaw askiy: Cree land

nêhiyawêwin: Cree words/language

nīcimos: my sweetheart, my lover

pēyak: one

pēyak nīso nisto: one two three

ACKNOWLEDGMENTS

Merci chok to Caitlin Ward for her careful and considerate editing work on this collection, and to Heather Dickson of Dickson Designs for the custom beadwork on the cover. Having two of my closest friends be such a significant a part of this journey was the best medicine I could ask for.

Thank you to Erica Lee and Brittany Catherine for early readings of this manuscript and for helping me finesse it into something more. Your constructive words, reflections, and joy over this manuscript made me see the possibilities within.

Thank you to Farris Lemaigre for the Dene translations, emerging from the community of La Loche, SK. Thank you to Bonnie Yew for the Cree translations, coming from Canoe Lake Cree First Nation, SK. And a special thank-you to my aunt Marge Reynolds, for the Dene syllabics, from English River First Nation, SK.

Thank you to Arsenal Pulp Press, and especially Shirarose, for believing in these poems and helping me finish this in a good way, for providing such a supportive and creative community, and for the endless patience with my endless questions.

Finally, a special merci chok to Joshua Whitehead, Eden Robinson, and Daniel Heath Justice for the time and care taken in speaking for this collection—you bougie ass bitches, I love you.

ARTIST STATEMENT: HEATHER DICKSON

When Tenille first approached me for the custom beadwork for *nedí nezu*, I was both excited and humbled. She and I have become best friends over the past few years, and we had spent many hours talking on the phone as she worked through both the relationships and the ensuing poetry written within this book. I knew that I wanted to create a piece that spoke to Tenille's personality—bright, engaging, colourful—as well as to the connection she has to the land and her community. Before I began beading, I thought about Tenille, trying to incorporate colours and patterns that reminded me of her. She had provided examples of her Grandmother Rose's beadwork to draw inspiration from, and we had spent some time talking about what made her think of home. I was reminded that we both share connotations of the idea of home through nature—we think of home and our lands, and we imagine wild roses, picking blueberries and cranberries, and the tiny wildflowers that grow abundant when you know where to look for them.

And then I began, as I always do, by shifting through the thousands of colours of beads in my collection, picking out hues and cuts that would eventually become part of the final piece. With colours such as honey and daffodil, crimson and garnet, rouge and rosewood, I would laugh and remember previous adventures I had shared with Tenille. Picking out lilacs and lavenders, azures and teals, and grounding the selection with the greens

119

shared in our lands—sage, moss, juniper, pine—it became a visual representation of Tenille and her stories. I used sizes eleven and fifteen, perfect for the details used within, and the type of beads included twenty-four-karat gold, silver, copper, lava stones, moonstones, abalone, Swarovski crystals, turquoise, and antique European beads.

I made sure to include her grandma's patterns of blue and purple florals in the middle of the piece, as well as my grandmother's floral beading pattern of the three little petal flowers, using both to represent the matriarchs in our lives. In the middle of the wild rose is abalone, representing the ocean and the time when Tenille lived in Vancouver, and there are turquoise beads representing connections to the Diné and her travels south. As a nod to her Dene heritage, there are two white beads within the leaves and the blue/purple flowers that match Grandmother Rose's beadwork patterns. I added the miniature flowers because they are the same colours used within the piece as a whole, and to me, these tiny florals are a visual representation of how Tenille's poetry inspires others, and how people can relate to it, taking little pieces for themselves—little pieces of joy, of laughter, of healing, of good medicine, for our communities to enjoy.

HEATHER DICKSON was born and raised in the Yukon. She is Tlingit from the Carcross/Tagish First Nation and Nuxalk Nation from Bella Coola, BC. Dickson received her diploma in fashion design at the Art Institute of Vancouver (now LaSalle College Vancouver) in 2010. However, her training began many years earlier, as she had been watching and learning the intricate art of beading since she was a child. Surrounded by rich Indigenous culture her whole life, she was always eager to learn traditional sewing and has been inspired by women from all over the North, resulting in teachings from the top of the Yukon to the bottom. Dickson has found a beautiful balance between her traditional and artisan skills and takes great pride in combining them within her business, Dickson Designs. This artistic balance provides her with a strong connection to her Indigenous heritage and keeps her rooted to her cultural identity in a modern world. *dicksonfashiondesigns.ca*

Photo credit: Emma Love

TENILLE K. CAMPBELL is a Dene/Metis author and photographer from English River First Nation in Treaty Ten, northern Saskatchewan. Her acclaimed debut poetry collection, *#Indian-LovePoems* (Signature Editions), was shortlisted for the Indigenous Voices Award. Campbell is the force behind sweetmoon photography, which specializes in capturing NDN joy in its many forms. She is also the co-creator and a blogger at *tea&bannock*, an online collective for Indigenous women photographers and artists to share their stories. Campbell completed her MFA in creative writing at the University of British Columbia and is working on a doctoral degree in Indigenous Literature at the University of Saskatchewan.

tenillecampbell.com